Contents

DISCARDED

D0334447

France: Unpacked

You've arrived in fabulous France, a country at the heart of Western Europe. France is about the size of Italy and the United Kingdom combined and is visited by more people (81.4 million in 2011) than any other country in the world. France has a long and fascinating history. It has given the world fine foods and wines, key ideas in philosophy, wonderful art and amazing advances in science. So, read on to learn more about France and its people; from the palace with 700 rooms to the Frenchman who ate an aeroplane!

Fact File

Area: 551,500km²
Population: 62,814,233
Capital city: Paris
Land Borders: 2,889km with eight countries

Currency: The Euro
National Symbol: Gallic Rooster

Flag:
The French flag is called the *tricolore*. Its colours were first used on a rosette during the French Revolution (see page 9).

Useful Phrases

Bonjour - Hello

Au revoir - Goodbye

S'il vous plaît - Please

Merci - Thank you

Je ne comprends pas - I don't understand

Je m'appelle - My name is

Est-ce que vous pouvez m'aider? - Can you help me?

Comment dit-on cela en français? - What is that called in French?

In 1954, the council of Châteauneuf-du-Pape made it illegal for flying saucers to land in the town.

Europe's largest sand dune, the Dune de Pilat, stands over 107m high, 500m wide and 2.7km long. It overlooks the Atlantic Ocean.

The French village with the shortest name is Y. It is found in the Somme region of northern France.

The City of Light

P aris is France's capital and one of the world's great cities. It started out as a small village called Lutetia but became the centre of the Frankish empire in the 6th century. Today it is a bustling centre of art, culture, finance, food and business. Hundreds of companies have their headquarters in the city. A fifth of the French population live in and around Paris, which exerts great influence on the rest of the country.

NO WAY!

To prevent the real city being bombed by German aircraft during World War I, a fake Paris was built out of wood to the north of the city!

In Seine

The original inhabitants of Paris were the Parisii tribe, who settled on the Île de la Cité, an island in the middle of the River Seine. This 776km-long river flows through the city dividing it into left and right banks. Many of Paris' most astonishing buildings are close to the Seine, including the impressive Louvre museum (home of the *Mona Lisa*) and the imposing Notre-Dame Cathedral.

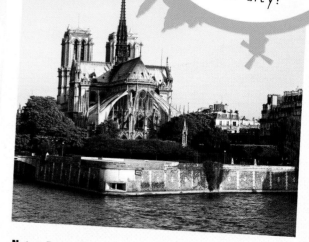

Notre-Dame Cathedral was completed in 1345. There's a 387-step climb to the top of its south tower.

The Eiffel Tower

The Eiffel Tower was only meant to be a temporary monument when it was completed in 1889. It is now one of the world's most recognisable landmarks and at 324m high is the tallest building in Paris. The huge steel framework is held together by 2.5 million rivets and requires over 60 tonnes of paint every seven years to prevent rust. More than 7 million people go up the tower every year.

The Eiffel Tower is lit up at night by 20,000 light bulbs.

Street cafés and restaurants line parts of the Avenue des Champs-Élysées.

Grand Avenues

In the mid-19th century, Baron Haussmann was employed to redesign much of central Paris. He transformed the narrow winding medieval alleyways into a network of broad streets, called avenues, heading out from the centre and linked by other streets known as boulevards. Today, some of these grand avenues are home to luxury fashion and clothing stores or pavement cafés.

Ruling France

Today, France is a republic. The President is elected by French adults voting in elections. He or she then appoints a Prime Minister, who appoints the government. In the past, France was ruled by kings and queens. The monarchy stretched back over 1,000 years to the Franks - a tribe of people who took France from the Romans and gave the country its name.

Bastille Day is now a national holiday in France with a large military parade in Paris and events all over France.

Kings and Queens

A long line of kings, many named Louis, ruled France for centuries. During the Middle Ages, French kings battled with England and other European states for territory and influence. Costly wars saw the country fall into debt. Extravagant King Louis XIV (1638-1715) built the biggest palace in Europe at Versailles, yet only took three baths in his whole life.

Louis XIV was known as the Sun King because it was said the whole of France revolved around him.

The National Razor

During and after the Revolution, thousands of nobles, including the king and queen, were executed. Many were beheaded by the sharp falling blade of the fearsome guillotine – nicknamed 'the national razor'. This deathly device was invented by a doctor from Paris and was supposed to slice the head off in one blow.

Revolution!

In the late 18th century France was torn apart by an uprising of ordinary people. They were tired of the lavish spending of rich people and the harsh laws and taxes imposed on them by their rulers King Louis XVI and his queen, Marie-Antoinette. On 14 July 1789, a mob of angry people stormed and captured the Bastille, an old royal prison in Paris, triggering the overthrow of the royalty.

 Marie-Antoinette's last words were an apology to her executioner for stepping on his foot!

Napoleon

Shortly after the Revolution, French military man Napoleon Bonaparte rose to power. He ruled France from 1799 to 1814, and declared himself Emperor in 1804. By 1812, he controlled much of central and eastern Europe. Bonaparte was eventually forced into exile by a series of military defeats including the decisive Battle of Waterloo in 1815. France was then ruled by a mixture of kings and emperors until 1871 when it became a republic.

Fruit of the Earth

France may no longer be a nation of farmers, but its half a million farms still employ almost 800,000 people directly. Over one third of France's land is given over to farming and makes up one sixth of all the farmland in the European Union. The country's large size, its mild range of climates and fertile soils allow it to produce huge amounts of crops and rear large numbers of livestock.

NO WAY!

In 2010, a single bottle of wine from Bordeaux, a Chateâu Cheval Blanc 1947 vintage, sold at auction for £192,000.

Wine Time

Grapes have been grown to make wine in France for over 2,500 years. Along with Italy, it is one of the world's biggest wine producers. All French regions, from Burgundy to the Loire, produce different types of wine due to the soil, climate conditions and the types of grapes grown. The famous Bordeaux region alone produces 850 million bottles of wine a year.

Most grape harvests take place in September.

Regional Specialities

Different regions of France are renowned for different products: from fruit orchards in the Garonne and Rhône valleys, to large crops of wheat and other cereals in the north and centre of the country. Cows and sheep are common in France, as are goats, whose milk is used to make cheese. Almost 300 million chickens, ducks and geese are reared every year in France, too.

A field of wheat in Burgundy. In 2011, French farms produced 38 million tonnes of wheat.

Rural Life

Sixty years ago, around a third of the population worked on farms. Since that time, many farms have been merged together so that farm machinery can do jobs more efficiently. Now, there are more than 1.2 million tractors at work in the country. Thousands of people have moved from the countryside to the cities, leaving some villages struggling whilst others have looked to attract tourists keen on sampling French rural life.

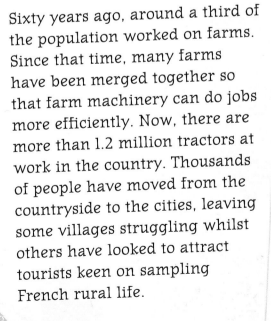

Home and Away

France is known as *l'hexagone* because of its roughly six-sided shape. It has three long coasts with the English Channel, Atlantic Ocean and Mediterranean Sea. At its greatest size it measures 965km north-to-south and around 935km east-to-west. The French are very proud of their language, which has given the English language hundreds of words, from menu and table to police, art and mountain. Today, over 220 million people worldwide speak French.

Language Laws

France was the first country to have an organisation to govern its language. The Académie Française was formed in 1635. Its 40 members, called immortals, produce an official dictionary and rule on matters of words and grammar. In recent times they have tried to influence the government to stop English words and phrases, including 'e-mail', 'best of' and 'car park', creeping into their language.

The Palais de l'Institut de France in Paris where the Académie Française is based.

Two women meet in Mali, a country of over 14.5 million people that gained independence from France in 1960.

Monaco

French is the official language of a tiny nation completely enclosed by mainland France. Monaco lies on the Mediterranean coast and was founded more than 700 years ago. It's tiny! At just 2.02km² it's about the same size as Britain's Alton Towers theme park. Yet more than 30,000 people live there, many of them are wealthy business people, movie stars or racing drivers taking advantage of Monaco's lack of income tax.

Luxury yachts and glitzy high rise apartments dominate the seafront of Monaco.

Far-flung Lands

In the past, France was a major colonial power with territory on every continent. French remains the official language of 29 independent countries, many in Africa, including Mali. French citizens living in overseas territories, including islands such as Martinique in the Caribbean and French Guiana in South America, also speak French. All these overseas departments, territories and collectives elect politicians to France's parliament.

NO WAY!

The French used to have strict rules about children's first names. In 1992, the rules were relaxed and the most common name that year was not Jacques or Jean-Paul but Kevin!

Power and Progress

France is one of the largest economic powers in the world. Its industries produce steel, chemicals and high-tech products from computer games to electrical goods. French car-makers including Peugeot, Citroen and Renault churn out more than 1.95 million vehicles a year. Michelin, whose headquarters are in Clermont-Ferrand, is the world's largest tyre maker, producing 150 million tyres per year.

Aerospace

France is a world leader in aviation and space technology. They produce Ariane rockets to launch satellites, many of which are also made in France. Based in Toulouse, Airbus is Europe's leading airliner producer. Its A380 aircraft is the world's biggest and is capable of carrying up to 853 passengers! Many aircraft are on show at the annual Paris Air Show – the world's oldest and largest air show, which includes spectacular flying displays.

Look up! A 72.7m long A380 airbus comes in to land at the Paris Air Show.

Large fields of sweet-smelling lavender in Provence, where it blooms from June to August.

Fine Fragrances

In medieval times, many French people used strong-smelling flowers like jasmine and lavender to mask the stink of unwashed bodies and a lack of flushing toilets. A massive perfume industry built up in France, especially in Paris and around the small town of Grasse in Provence where many fragrant plants were grown. Today, giant French perfume and beauty companies like Chanel, Dior and L'Oréal produce thousands of expensive perfumes. Chanel's Grand Extrait perfume, for example, was launched in 2013 and costs over £2,700 a bottle.

These nuclear reactors at Tricastin in southeastern France generate about 6% of the country's electricity.

NO WAY!

Liliane Bettencourt, heiress of the perfume and beauty company, L'Oréal, is France's richest woman!

Gone Nuclear

France generates more of its electricity using nuclear power than any other country in the world. The country has more than 50 nuclear power stations that generate 78% of all its electricity. Nuclear power helps give the French population some of the cheapest electricity in Europe but many are concerned about its safety and campaign for alternative energies to be used.

Grand Designs

From astonishing bridges to lavish palaces and cathedrals, French architecture is often breathtaking!

Chartres Cathedral

Built in the 13th century, this enormous 130m-long cathedral is made of limestone and is a prime example of gothic architecture. Chartres has an 113m-high northwest tower, more than a hundred stone sculptures and most of its stunning 176 stained glass windows are original. The glass was removed carefully and stored during World War II.

Chartres Cathedral draws around 2 million visitors every year.

Versailles

When Louis XIV decided to build his palace outside of Paris, he didn't skimp. He turned his father's hunting lodge at Versailles into the grandest royal home Europe had ever seen. The palace featured 700 rooms, 2,000 windows, 67 staircases and 1,200 fireplaces. Outside, the sculptured gardens – containing about 200,000 trees – were four times the size of Monaco (see p.13).

The Hall of Mirrors at Versailles contains 357 mirrors and over 40 chandeliers.

Colour-coding at the Pompidou Centre – plumbing in green, air shafts in blue and electrical wiring in yellow.

Pipe Dreams

Named after Georges Pompidou, the 19th President of France, the giant Pompidou Centre holds a huge public library, Europe's biggest modern art museum and a centre for research into sound. The centre is very striking as its infrastructure, such as water pipes and ventilation ducts, runs on the outside of the building. Although it caused an outrage when it was opened in 1977, Parisians have since grown to love it.

Building Bridges

This astonishing bridge is not to be crossed if you're afraid of heights. The Millau Viaduct was constructed to span the Tarn Valley and provide a quick route from southern France into Spain. It's a dizzying 270m from the road deck to the ground below. Opened in 2004, the whole structure is made mostly of concrete and weighs a hefty 290,000 tonnes.

Up to 25,000 cars cross the Millau Viaduct every day.

NO WAY!

During Louis XIV's reign, it's thought that a fifth of France's entire spending was just on running the palace at Versailles.

Bon Appetit

France is a nation of food lovers. Top chefs, such as Paul Bocuse and Alain Ducasse, are treated like superstars, and French cuisine has influenced what people eat in many other countries. In general, the French consume less processed food than other nations, preferring to make their own dishes from fresh ingredients - although fast food sales are rising amongst the young.

Fine dining is all about taste, technique and presentation.

Fine Dining

Both Paris and other cities think of themselves as the food capitals of France. Each have their own speciality dishes. The city of Lyons, for example, is famous for its wide range of cooked meats, pâtés and special sausages often served at small, friendly restaurants called *bouchons*. Paris is home to as many as 13,000 restaurants, from simple bistros to luxury restaurants where a full meal with wine can cost more than 300 euros each.

Extreme Eats

Truffles

Do the French really eat snails and frogs' legs? Yes they do! Some also eat sea urchins and a dish called *steak tartare*, which is finely chopped beef or horse meat eaten raw. Some of the most highly-prized ingredients in France are truffles, a species of strong-tasting underground fungi, related to mushrooms. These are sniffed out by trained dogs or pigs handled by expert truffle hunters, known as *trufficulteurs*. Some truffles can sell for more than £1000 per kilo.

These *escargot* (snails) are cooked with garlic. Mmmmm.

NO WAY!

Michel Lotito - known as Monsieur Mangetout (Mr Eats Everything) - ate metal and glass objects from bicycles to light bulbs. In 1978-80, he consumed a whole Cessna light aircraft piece by piece. Don't try this at home!

Say Cheese

No one eats more cheese than the French – an estimated 26kg per person every year. Sheep, goats' and cows' milk are all used to make more than 400 different cheeses. Every region of France is proud of its own local cheeses, from Normandy's Camembert to the Loire's Port Salut. Comté, produced in eastern France, is the country's most popular cheese with around 40,000 tonnes made every year.

A selection of mouthwatering French cheeses on display in a shop in Provence.

The Arts

France is well known for its artistic reputation, producing many great authors, playwrights, sculptors and painters. French musicians, too, have found world renown, from classical composers such as George Bizet, Maurice Ravel and Claude Debussy, to modern music acts such as Daft Punk.

The Blue Dancers by French Impressionist, Edgar Degas.

Making an Impression

One of French art's most influential movements was Impressionism. This began amongst a group of Parisian artists in the 19th century, who started using bold colours and brushstrokes to represent the natural effects of light on scenes of everyday life. This new style shocked many at the time but also became popular and influenced other artists. Works by Impressionists, such as Claude Monet and Edgar Degas amongst others, are still viewed by millions at French galleries and museums.

French Film

Cinema was born in France! In 1895, the Lumière brothers, Auguste and Louis, first started showing films they had made to audiences in Paris using their own design of camera and projector. Since then, French film directors including Jean-Luc Godard and François Truffaut, and actors such as Gérard Depardieu and Audrey Tautou have achieved international stardom. Every year, the French town of Cannes hosts an important film festival which attracts movie-makers and famous actors from Hollywood and beyond.

NO WAY!

French writer Georges Perecs' 1969 novel, *La Disparition*, was written without using the letter 'e' anywhere in its 300 pages!

By the Book

From Voltaire and Émile Zola to Jules Verne and Marcel Proust, France has produced many influential writers. But few were as popular with ordinary people as Victor Hugo, who wrote *Les Misérables* and *The Hunchback of Notre Dame*. When he died in 1885, an incredible two million people followed his funeral procession. Many classic French children's books still thrill today, including *The Three Musketeers* by Alexandre Dumas and *Cinderella* and *Sleeping Beauty*, retold by Charles Perrault. The comic book character Asterix is a French favourite as well.

Asterix first appeared in 1961 and has since starred in a dozen films and in books which have sold more than 325 million copies.

En Vacance

You already know that millions of foreigners visit France each year, but where do the French go *en vacance* (on holiday) themselves? The surprising answer is... France! The majority of French people holiday by visiting other parts of their large country.

NO WAY!

In 2011/12, more people skied in France than any other country - a total of 55.3 million skier days.

Getting Around

Holiday time in France can see France's 12,000km of motorways, known as *Autoroutes*, crowded with vehicles, so many French people hop on the TGV (*Train à Grande Vitesse*) high-speed rail network. Around 127 million passengers took the TGV in 2012. Some holidaymakers head for the countryside, staying in holiday homes known as *gîtes* or camping with their families. Others stay at *colonies de vacances* (holiday camps). While on holiday, many people like to hike or cycle through France's forests and hills.

TGVs can reach speeds of up to 320km/h. The first TGV train travelled almost 1 million km during testing.

Arrive early to grab a spot on Nice's beautiful beaches in summer.

Life's a Beach

Along France's long Mediterranean coast are a number of harbour cities such as Marseilles and Nice. There are also sandy beaches in the west, and rocky coves and pebble beaches in the eastern part, the latter known as the French Riviera. Here, world-famous resorts such as St-Raphaël and St-Tropez are crammed with holiday-makers. Even the chillier Atlantic Ocean waters of France's west coast attract many visitors lured by surfing, seeing the sites and tasting local seafood such as oysters.

Winter Retreats

The French are huge winter sports fans and with the most ski resorts in a single country on their doorstep, who can blame them? The French portion of the Alps mountain range in the southeast of the country contains over 3,700 ski lifts, more than any other nation, carrying skiers and snowboarders up its many slopes. One ski area, Les Trois Vallées (The Three Valleys), contains over 330 different ski slopes.

A skier carves down fresh powder in one of France's ski resorts in the Alps.

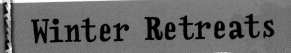

Made in France

Did you hear about the French car engineer who invented the bikini or the champion tennis player who invented the polo shirt? What about the French chemist who made margarine or the mathematician who invented the pencil sharpener? Here are some more ingenious French inventions...

Up, Up and Away

In September 1783, a rooster, a sheep and a duck took to the air in a hot air balloon built by the Montgolfier brothers, Joseph-Michel and Jacques-Étienne. The eight-minute-long flight was watched by the king, Louis XVI, and was followed two months later by the first manned flight.

Breathing Under Water

Jacques Cousteau tested the first successful aqua-lung off the coast of the French Riviera in 1943. It featured an air tank worn on the diver's back that fed air through a special valve, which stopped damage to the diver's lungs.

Louis Braille

Louis Braille (1809-53) was just 15 years old when he devised a system of reading for people who were visually impaired. It used a pattern of raised dots on the page to represent each letter, number and punctuation mark. Braille is used by millions of people around the world today.

Bright Lights

Georges Claude, a French chemist, invented neon lighting in 1910. He demonstrated that neon gas is sensitive to electricity and glows when heated. Shops, cafés and bars use neon lighting today to display their names in glowing letters.

REPUBLIQUE CENTRAFRICAINE
PASTEUR
Centenaire du premier vaccin contre la Rage
POSTES 1985
150F

Fighting Disease

Louis Pasteur was a pioneer of fighting infectious diseases. Thousands of lives have been saved by the Pasteur Institute, which opened in Paris in 1888 and created vaccines to prevent diseases like polio, diphtheria and yellow fever.

Stethoscope

The stethoscope is a device for listening to the inner workings of the body. The first design was made of wood and looked like a small ear trumpet. It was invented in 1816 by René Laennec.

Polo Shirt

The French, seven-time Grand Slam Tennis champ René Lacoste designed the polo shirt in 1926 because the tennis whites of the times were uncomfortable and restricted movement.

NO WAY!

One French invention that didn't catch on was the car shovel. It was a large, basket-shaped scoop fitted to the front of a car to catch pedestrians and lift them out of the way!

Allez Sport

France is one of the world's great sporting powers. It has won 671 Summer Olympics medals and 94 Winter Games medals. One of the four biggest tennis tournaments in the world, the French Open, is held in Paris every year. Other popular French sports include athletics, handball, basketball, skiing, sailing and *pétanque* - a game similar to boules or bowls.

French Football

FIFA, the organisation that runs world football, was founded in France in 1904 and it was a French football official, Jules Rimet, who suggested the idea of the World Cup. France won the competition in 1998 and finished runner-up in 2006. French football teams have also won the European Championships twice (1984, 2000) and the Olympics (1984). Famous French clubs like Marseilles, Paris Saint Germain and Lyon play in Ligue 1, the top division of football in France.

Franck Ribéry has played for five French clubs including Metz and Marseilles.

Tour de France

Every June, the country hosts the world's biggest cycle race – the Tour de France. This three-week test of cyclists' strength, speed and endurance sees competitors push themselves to the limit. They race up and down steep mountains, around treacherous turns and through rapid sprint stages. Some Tours include stages in other European countries such as Italy, England and Belgium. The 2013 race was the 100th Tour and was 3,360km long. It started on the French island of Corsica and then travelled all over France, finishing in Paris.

Each competitor hopes to get the honour of wearing the yellow jersey that signifies the race leader.

NO WAY!

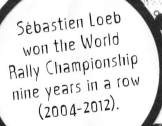

Sébastien Loeb won the World Rally Championship nine years in a row (2004-2012).

Le Mans

This 24-hour car race takes place in June each year, in the town of Le Mans in northern France. Around 50 cars race round the track for 24 hours straight trying to complete the most laps in the time allowed. In the 2012 race, the winning team drove 5151.76km – that's like driving from London to Paris 16 times!

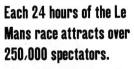

Each 24 hours of the Le Mans race attracts over 250,000 spectators.

Life in France

When French adults meet, they're more likely to ask each other about their interests and leisure time than about their work. Most French people believe in living a pleasant lifestyle with relatively short working hours and plenty of time and income spent on their wellbeing – known as *bien-être*. This often translates into good clothes, good food, leisurely mealtimes and long holidays!

Going to School

Lunch breaks are long at school – up to two hours! Until 2008, the French school week ran from Monday to Saturday with part or all of Wednesdays off. Now, it's Monday to Friday. At 15, children go to a *lycée*, similar to a high school, for up to three years. At 17 or 18, they sit an exam called a *baccalauréat* which involves tests on around 10 school subjects. Passing your 'bac' is thought to be essential if you want to go to university or enter a well-paid professional career.

A *maîtresse* (female primary school teacher) helps a girl in her class.

 The Galeries Lafayette, a 10-storey-high luxury department store in Paris. In 2009, it sold one billion euros worth of goods.

Looking Good, Living Well

A 2011 survey of 34 wealthy countries of the world found that the French sleep, eat and shop the longest of all nations. Queuing at a *boulangerie* for just-baked bread or at a *pâtisserie* for a delightful sweet cake is a daily pleasure not a chore for many French people. They are also very fashion-conscious and tend to dress smartly most of the time.

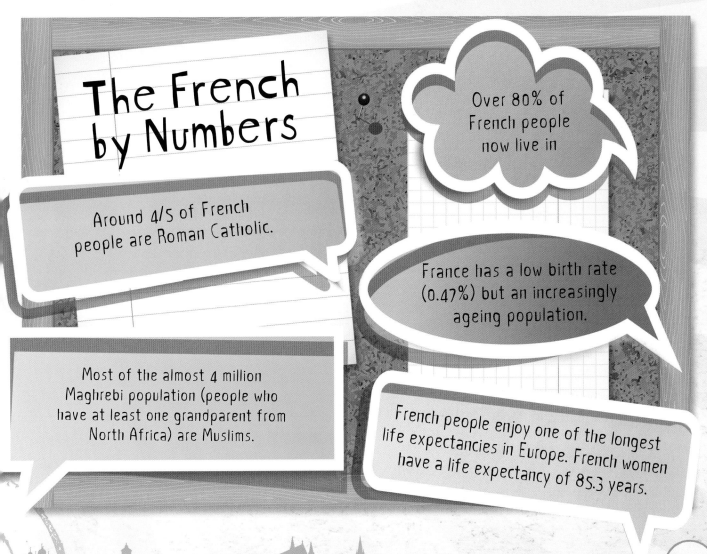

The French by Numbers

Around 4/5 of French people are Roman Catholic.

Most of the almost 4 million Maghrebi population (people who have at least one grandparent from North Africa) are Muslims.

Over 80% of French people now live in

France has a low birth rate (0.47%) but an increasingly ageing population.

French people enjoy one of the longest life expectancies in Europe. French women have a life expectancy of 85.3 years.

More Information

Websites

http://www.tour-eiffel.fr/images/PDF/all_you_need_to_know_about_the_eiffel_tower.pdf
All the facts about the Eiffel Tower and events that have occurred there.

http://www.frenchaffair.com.au/fun/proverbs.htm
A fun and handy collection of popular French sayings with their English equivalents.

http://www.bonjourlafrance.com/french-food/french-recipes/french-desserts/french-toast.htm
A website packed with easy-to-make authentic French recipes.

http://www.guardian.co.uk/film/2011/mar/22/french-cinema-short-history
A short history of French cinema with video clips.

Apps
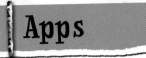

Fotopedia France A wide and varied selection of groovy photos and facts about France for your iPhone or iPad.

French Belote Enjoy playing the traditional French card game Belote with this free Android app.

Musée du Louvre This official app from the Louvre Museum details over 100 of its exhibits.

Versailles A free app about the grand palace for both Android and iPhones is available from: http://en.chateauversailles.fr/application-iphone-en

Movies

Coco Before Chanel (PG 13) A biopic about Gabrielle 'Coco' Chanel, a legendary French fashion designer, from her poor upbringing in an orphanage in Auvergne to her rise to the top of Paris fashion.

The Red Balloon (U)
This simple, short, charming film is about a boy and his balloon. It was directed by Albert Lamorisse and won an Oscar in the 1950s.

Clips

http://www.completefrance.com/videos
France magazine has a channel of videos on all sorts of French subjects from the oldest bakery in Paris to extreme sports in the Alps.

http://www.youtube.com/playlist?list=PL7BC880B8B70AB2CB
Watch five videos on the Tour de France's greatest moments brought to you by ITV.

http://www.youtube.com/watch?v=CUrEJBsWLfA
Watch an epic documentary about Louis XIV, Marie Antoinette and the French Revolution.

http://dsc.discovery.com/tv-shows/other-shows/videos/discovery-atlas-france-geography.htm
The geography of France shown in stunning fashion by the Discovery Channel.

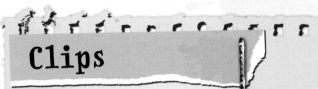

Books

Fact Cat: Countries: France by Alice Harman
(Wayland, 2014)

Discover Countries: France by Susan Crean
(Wayland, 2011)

Extraordinary Lives: Napoleon by Judith Anderson
(Wayland, 2010)

The Real: France by Anne-Marie Laval
(Franklin Watts, 2013)

To say something will never happen - like 'when pigs fly' in English - the French say, 'Quand les poules auront les dents' in French. This literally means, 'when hens have teeth!'

Glossary

alternative energies – Forms of energy, such as solar power and wind power, that do not burn fossil fuels, such as coal or oil, and do not use nuclear power.

bistro – A small restaurant usually selling lower priced meals and dishes.

cathedral – A Christian church that is the seat or base of a bishop (a senior figure in the church).

fertile – Soil or conditions good for growing plants and crops in.

grand slam – In tennis, the name given to the four most highly-prized tournaments each year: the French Open, Australian Open, US Open and Wimbledon.

income tax – A sum of money that each person pays to the government out of what they earn.

inhabitants – People who live in a place.

nuclear power – The splitting of atoms to generate electricity in nuclear power stations.

processed food – Packaged food made in factories, such as ready meals and frozen pizzas, designed to be quickly and easily cooked or prepared by people.

projector – A device used to display photos or moving pictures on a screen.

republic – A form of government without a king or queen in charge, where the population vote to elect the people who run their country.

resort – A location that is a popular place to go for leisure time or for holidays.

vaccine – A substance given to a patient to help their body to fight a certain disease.

viaduct – A long structure, similar to a bridge, carrying a road deck.

Index